Chinese Pronunciation and Tones

Consonants

The Chinese consonants **b, d, f, g, h, k, l, m, n, p, s, t, w, y** are all pronounced as in English. The other consonants are pronounced as follows:

Examples:

c	like English *ts* in "its"	餐 **cān** (meal)
j	like English *j* in "jeer"	鸡 **jī** (chicken)
q	like English *ch* in "cheap"	千 **qiān** (thousand)
r	like English *ur* in "sure"	人 **rén** (person)
x	like English *sh* "sheet"	希 **xī** (hope)
z	like English *ds* in "kids"	早 **zǎo** (early)
ch	like English *ch* in "church"	吃 **chī** (to eat)
sh	like English *sh* in "shot"	烧 **shāo** (to burn)
zh	like English *dg* in "edge"	真 **zhēn** (real, true)

Vowels

The Chinese vowels are pronounced as follows:

Examples:

a	like English *a* in "far"	妈 **mā** (mother)
e	like English *e* in "per"	二 **èr** (two)
i	like English *ee* in "gee"	一 **yī** (one)
o	like English *o* in "or"	抹 **mǒ** (touch)
u	like English *oo* in "sooth"	雨 **yǔ** (rain)
ü	like French *u* and German *ü*	绿 **lǜ** (green)

Tones

A tone refers to the variation in pitch in the pronunciation of a syllable. There are basically 4 tones each marked by a different diacritic:

First tone: **mā** (mom/mommy)   Third tone: **mǎ** (a horse)
Second tone: **má** (hemp)   Fourth tone: **mà** (to scold)

Tone chart

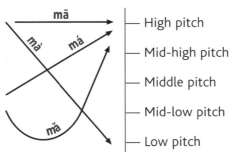

There is also a neutral tone which is spoken light and soft, and has no discritical mark. It occurs frequently when a syllable is reduplicated, for example, **bàba** (father), or in the second syllable of certain Chinese words, for example, **tāde** (his/hers).

1

Common Greetings and Expressions 🎧

The following are some common expressions used for daily communication, or for special occasions.

你(您)好！ **Nǐ (nín) hǎo!** Hello! How're you?

早上好！ **Zǎoshàng hǎo!** Good morning.

下午好！ **Xiàwǔ hǎo!** Good afternoon.

午餐吃过吗？ **Wǔcān chīguò ma?** Have you had your lunch?

好高兴认识你们。 **Hǎo gāoxīng rènshi nǐmen!** Very happy to know you.

久仰大名！ **Jiǔyǎng dàmíng!** I have been looking forward to meeting you for a long time. (more formal)

你贵姓！ **Nǐ guì xìng!** What is your (honorable last) name?

你叫什么名字？ **Nǐ jiào shénme míngzi?** What is your name? (informal)

你们家有什么人？ **Nǐmen jiā yǒu shénme rén?** Who is in your family?

他多大？／他几岁？ **Tā duō dà? / Tā jǐ suì?** How old is he?

你在哪儿工作？ **Nǐ zài nǎr gōngzuò?** Where do you work?

请多多指教。 **Qǐng duōduo zhǐjiào.** Please guide me.

好久不见了！您还好吗？ **Hǎo jiǔ bújiàn le! Nín hái hǎo ma?** Long time no see! How've you been?

→老样子。 **Lǎo yàngzi.** Same as before.

最近怎么样？忙不忙？ **Zuìjìn zěnmeyàng? Mángbumáng?** How have you been recently? Busy?

→还可以。 **Hái kěyǐ.** I'm fine.

你来自哪里？ **Nǐ láizì nǎli?** Where do you come from?

你是哪国人？ **Nǐ shì nǎguó rén?** Which country are you from?

欢迎，欢迎！ **Huānyíng, huānyíng!** Welcome, welcome!

请进。 **Qǐng jìn.** Please come in.

再见/拜拜！ **Zàijiàn/Bàibai!** Goodbye!

明天见！／回头见！ **Míngtiān jiàn!/Huítóu jiàn!** See you tomorrow/another time.

→后会有期。 **Hòuhuì yǒu qī.** We will meet another time.

慢走。 **Màn zǒu.** Safe travel.

祝你早日康复！ **Zhù nǐ zǎorì kāngfù!** Wishing you a speedy recovery.

喂(on the phone) **Wèi!** Hello.

可以说得慢一点吗？ **Kěyǐ shuōde màn yìdiǎn ma?** Could you speak more slowly?

这是什么意思？ **Zhèi shì shénme yìsi?** What does this mean?

这东西要多少钱？ **Zhèi dōngxi yào duōshao qián?** How much does this item cost?

请问，去最近的早市怎么走？ **Qǐng wèn, qù zuìjìnde zǎoshì zěnme zǒu?** Excuse me, how do I get to the nearest supermarket?

请稍等一下。 **Qǐng shāo děng yíxià.** Please wait a while.

不客气。 **Búkèqì.** Don't mention it.

了不起。 **Liǎobùqǐ.** Amazing/Awesome.

太酷吧！ **Tài kù ba.** That's cool.

今天天气预报怎么说？ **Jīntiān tiānqì yùbào zěnme shuō?** What is the weather forecast for today?

可以帮个忙吗？ **Kěyǐ bāng ge máng ma?** Could you help me?

麻烦你了。 **Máfan nǐle.** Sorry to bother you.

谢谢。 **Xièxie.** Thank you.

非常感谢！ **Fēicháng gǎnxiè!** Thank you so much!

恭喜恭喜！ **Gōngxǐ gōngxǐ!** Congratulations!

生日快乐。 **Shēngrì kuàilè!** Happy Birthday!

新年快乐！ **Xīnnián kuàilè!** Happy New Year!

恭喜发财！ **Gōngxǐ fācái!** May you be prosperous! (usually used at Chinese New Year)

祝你好运！ **Zhùnǐ hǎoyùn!** Good luck!

How to Write Chinese Characters

When you use a pencil, pen or brush to write Chinese characters, you form the lines, dots and hooks one step at a time in a particular direction and sequence. Although they may seem complicated at first, Chinese characters are composed of just eight basic strokes and their variations. Each stroke has its own name and a method of forming it. Please refer to the table below to learn the eight basic strokes and how to form them.

The Eight Basic Strokes

Stroke	Name of stroke	Instructions for writing	Examples	Variations of basic strokes in characters
一	horizontal stroke 横 **héng**	start from the left and continue the stroke to the right	二	
丨	vertical stroke 竖 **shù**	start from the top and end at the bottom, maintaining a straight stroke	你	中
丿	downward-left stroke 撇 **piě**	start from the right and move toward the lower left	人	千师
乀	downward-right stroke 捺 **nà**	start from the left and move to the bottom right	大	过
丶	dot 点 **diǎn**	start from the left and end at the lower right	学	心
㇀	upward stroke 提 **tí**	start from the bottom left and move toward the upper-right	习	酒
亅	hook stroke 钩 **gōu**	a line with a tiny hook at the end	小	长子戈
𠃌	turning stroke 折 **zhé**	start from the left, turn right	国	口匹

An Example of a Character with All Eight Basic Strokes

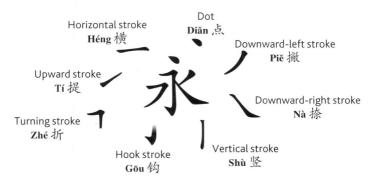

Horizontal stroke Héng 横
Dot Diǎn 点
Downward-left stroke Piě 撇
Upward stroke Tí 提
Downward-right stroke Nà 捺
Turning stroke Zhé 折
Hook stroke Gōu 钩
Vertical stroke Shù 竖

Learn to recognize and become familiar with each individual stroke. The direction, angle, length and order of writing the strokes are all important. Whether the character is simple or complex, comprised of just a few strokes or many, your ability to write Chinese characters will improve if you pay attention to these things. Practice writing each character many times in the correct way while pronouncing the character. By doing this, you will also be memorizing it.

Stroke Order and Rules

Throughout the years, rules have developed for writing Chinese characters. These rules help you in learning the correct formation of characters. It doesn't matter whether you are right handed or left handed. If you follow the rules for stroke order, you will be able to write beautiful Chinese characters.

Here are the main stroke order rules for forming Chinese characters. These general rules will help you understand more specific stroke order rules later on.

1. From top to bottom   **2. From left to right**

3. First the horizontal, then the vertical (as in the first 2 strokes)

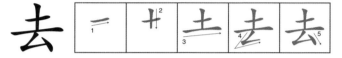

4. The down-stroke on the left before the one on the right

5. The enclosing strokes first, then the enclosed and finally the sealing stroke

6. The middle stroke before those on both sides

7. Left-falling stroke before right-falling stroke (as in the last 2 strokes)

Following these simple rules will help you write any character you encounter even if you have never seen it before. Just remember to form the strokes correctly and in the right order. Correct stroke formation and stroke order will become second nature to you if you practice writing the characters correctly from the start. Practice tracing the 48 characters on the next six pages. Follow the arrows and trace over the lines provided. Then practice writing them freehand.

How to Write 48 Basic Characters

人						
rén person; people						

儿						
ér/r child; suffix						

七						
qī seven						

八						
bā eight						

九						
jiǔ nine						

十						
shí ten						

三						
sān three						

个						
ge most common measure word						

女													
nǚ female	ㄑ	女	女	女	女	女							

子													
zǐ/zi son; seed; suffix	フ	了	子	子	子	子							

五													
wǔ five	一	丆	五	五	五	五	五						

六													
liù six	丶	二	六	六	六	六	六						

也													
yě also; too	フ	也	也	也	也	也							

少													
shǎo/shào few; little; young	丨	小	小	少	少	少	少						

日													
rì day	丨	冂	日	日	日	日	日						

月													
yuè month; moon	丿	月	月	月	月	月	月						

四													
sì four	丨	冂	叼	四	四	四	四	四					

他													
tā he	丿	亻	仂	他	他	他	他	他					

们													
men plural suffix (for persons)	丿	亻	亻	们	们	们	们	们					

叫													
jiào to call; shout	丨	口	口	叫	叫	叫	叫	叫					

生													
shēng to give birth; raw	丿	仁	仨	生	生	生	生	生					

名													
míng name	丿	夕	夕	夕	名	名	名	名	名				

字													
zì written character	丶	宀	宁	字	字	字	字	字	字				

吗													
ma question particle	丨	口	口	叩	吗	吗	吗	吗	吗				

多												
duō many, much												

妈												
mā mother												

年												
nián year												

好												
hǎo/hào good; alright												

吃												
chī to eat												

问												
wèn to ask												

不												
bù/bú not; no												

老												
lǎo old												

我													
wǒ I; me	亅	二	于	手	我	我	我	我	我	我			

男													
nán male	丨	冂	日	曲	田	男	男	男	男	男			

饭													
fàn meal; cooked rice	丿	勹	饣	饣	饤	饭	饭	饭	饭	饭			

弟													
dì younger brother	丶	丷	肖	肖	肖	弟	弟	弟	弟	弟			

姓													
xìng surname	乚	女	女	女	女	妒	姓	姓	姓	姓			

学													
xué to learn	丶	丷	丷	川	学	学	学	学	学	学			

爸													
bà father	丿	八	少	父	爷	爸	爸	爸	爸	爸			

姐													
jiě older sister	乚	女	女	如	姐	姐	姐	姐	姐	姐			

9

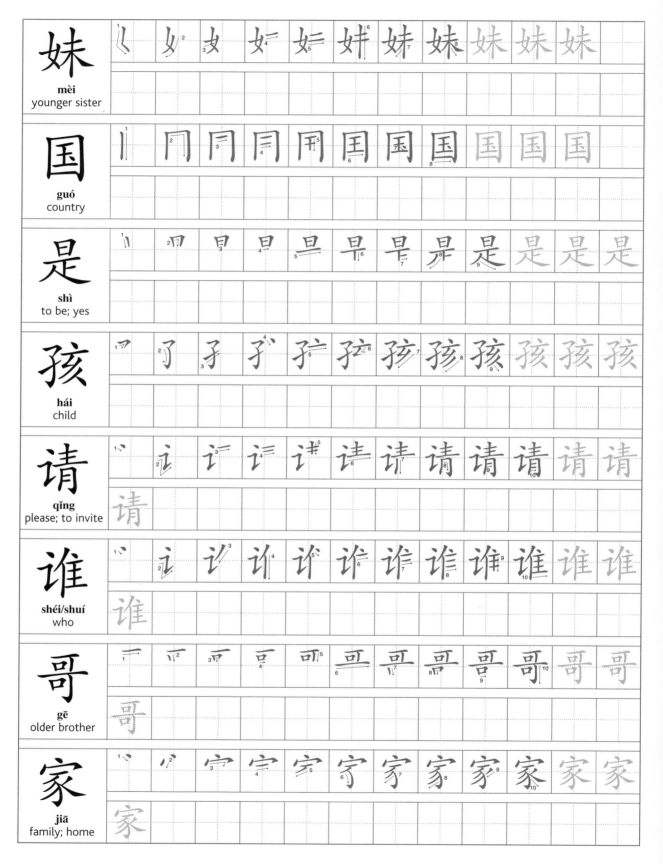

妹
mèi
younger sister

国
guó
country

是
shì
to be; yes

孩
hái
child

请
qǐng
please; to invite

谁
shéi/shuí
who

哥
gē
older brother

家
jiā
family; home

10

How Chinese Characters Work

The Three Elements of a Character

Chinese characters vary widely in their number of strokes, but they all occupy the same square space, and each one is pronounced in one syllable. Each character is made up of three basic elements: form (形), sound (音) and meaning (义). For example:

"我" is the form; and "**wǒ**" is the sound; and "I" is the meaning.

Over time, there have been many changes in the phonetics of Chinese characters. The composition and meanings, however, have remained somewhat the same. As a result, many Chinese people today can read ancient texts without much difficulty.

Before the inception of Chinese characters, communication was difficult within China due to the number of vastly different dialects being spoken. Chinese characters gave people a common ground for understanding.

How Characters are Formed

Traditional Chinese scholars grouped Chinese characters into six different types depending on the principle by which they were formed. We will only describe the four commonly known types here.

1. **Pictographs:** These characters were created by drawing pictures of objects. Over time the characters evolved from pictures into symbols which became standardized, then simplified to make writing easier. Pictographs tend to be quite simple, but some also appear as components or radicals in more complex characters.

木 **mù**   means "tree" or "wood"

山 **shān**   means "mountain"

雨 **yù**   means "rain"

月 **yuè**   means "moon"

2. **Ideographs:** These characters are iconic forms that illustrate abstract concepts. Characters that represent certain single digit numbers are in this category.

一 **yī** for "one"

二 **èr** for "two"

三 **sān** for "three"

The characters for "up" and "down" are also in this category. These two characters were originally written with a dot above and below a line.

上 **shàng** for "up" and 下 **xià** for "down".

3. **Compound ideographs:** These characters are composed of two components to represent an idea, for example:

小 (**xiǎo** "small") + 大 (**dà** "large") = 尖 (**jiān** "sharp")

人 (**rén** "person") + 木 (**mù** "tree") = 休 (**xiū** "to rest")

4. **Phono-semantic compounds:** Over 80% of Chinese characters fall into this category. These characters are composed of two components, one signifying its sound and the other signifying its meaning, for example:

女 (**nǚ** "woman") + 马 (**mǎ** "horse") = 妈 (**mā** "mother")

虫 (**chóng** "insect") + 文 (**wén** "literature") = 蚊 (**wén** "mosquito")

Composed Characters with New Meanings

In the Chinese language, many characters are composed of two or more simpler characters. When the simpler characters are joined together, the meaning and pronunciation of the new character is normally very different. There are twelve different ways to combine simple Chinese characters to make more complex ones. Here are just a few examples:

from top to bottom: 口 + 力 = 另

from left to right: 土 + 也 = 地

from left to middle to right:
言 (讠) + 身 + 寸 = 谢 and so on.

Chinese Radicals

A Chinese "radical" is an important component of each character that helps you to identify its meaning. It is sometimes considered a "classifier" since all characters that share a particular radical have meanings that are related in some way, and therefore form a "semantic class" or "grouping" of characters.

For example, the characters 吗 **ma** and 吃 **chī** both share the radical 口 **kǒu** which means "mouth" and therefore you know they have something to do with speaking or eating. And the characters 妈 **mā** and 她 **tā** both have the radical 女 **nǚ** which means "woman" and therefore they have to do with the female gender. The radicals themselves are often characters that can be used on their own. However, when they are used as part of another character as a radical, their shape is often changed in some way. Here are some examples:

人 turns into 亻 as a radical for 你, 他, and 们.
言 changes to 讠 as a radical for 说, 话, and 读.
水 becomes 氵 as a radical for 沙, 河, and 湖.

Common Radicals

Radicals	Meaning	Examples
亻	person	你，他，们，体，作，修，仁，低
女	woman	妈，姐，她，奶，妹，好，姑
讠	speech	说，话，语，订，讲，请，认，试
氵	water	汉，河，漂，汗，泪，浪，江，汽
彳	step	得，往，彼，行，街，很，微，待
纟	coil	红，绿，纱，级，纪，约，纸，组
木	wood	样，校，树，村，杯，朵，李，查
宀	roof	家，字，宝，安，完，客，室，宾
口	mouth	吃，喝，唱，右，吹，告，呼，品

Radicals	Meaning	Examples
日	sun	明，昨，晴，是，昏，时，晒，星
阝 (right)	city	那，都，邦，部，邻，邮，郊，郎
阝 (left)	mound	院，陈，阴，附，阶，阻，陪，队
辶	walk	这，边，还，进，连，运，送，追
艹	grass	茶，苹，菜，花，节，草，黄，药
心	heart	必，忠，怎，您，想，念，思，感
月	moon	有，服，朋，背，胆，肚，肥，育
土	earth	场，坏，至，城，在，幸，堂，墙
大	big	夫，买，奇，太，头，奖，套，夺
扌	hand	打，扔，扮，把，挡，抓，指，损

These are only a few examples to give you a general idea. Chinese radicals appear in various positions within characters. Some radicals appear on the left side of the character, e.g. 你, 他, 们, while other radicals appear on the right side of the character, e.g. 都, 那, 邓. Some radicals appear at the top of a character, e.g. 茶, 菜, 花, while other radicals appear at the bottom of a character, e.g. 名, 合, 右. As you learn more Chinese characters, you will learn to recognize the radicals in their various positions. Recognizing the radicals will also help you increase your vocabulary quickly.

Traditional vs Simplified Characters

With the growing importance of China, most people now learn the Chinese simplified characters that are the result of the Chinese government's efforts since the 1950s to simplify the characters into more manageable forms (with fewer strokes) rather than learning the older traditional forms.

Examples of characters before and after simplification:

Traditional	Simplified	Traditional	Simplified	Traditional	Simplified	Traditional	Simplified
還	还	聽	听	開	开	邊	边
請	请	響	响	賣	卖	臉	脸
來	来	氣	气	講	讲	覺	觉
萬	万	車	车	週	周	錯	错
興	兴	話	话	臨	临	幫	帮
紅	红	點	点	機	机	雞	鸡
貨	货	腦	脑	節	节	歡	欢
傘	伞	視	视	對	对	電	电
時	时	國	国	會	会	錢	钱
愛	爱	學	学	塊	块	養	养

Most countries now use simplified characters because they are the standard in China. Only Taiwan, Hong Kong and Macau continue to use traditional characters.

Basic Chinese Sentence Construction 🎧

- A basic Chinese sentence follows this order:
  Subject + verb + object

EXAMPLES:

我 会 写 汉字。 **Wǒ huì xiě Hànzì.**
I can write Chinese characters.

他们 喜欢 吃 水果。
Tāmén xǐhuan chī shuǐguǒ.
They like fruits.

- To ask a question, use 吗 **ma** for the ending.

EXAMPLE:

他去过中国吗?
Tā qù guò Zhōngguó ma?
Has he ever been to China?

Another way of asking questions is to use the yes/no (是不是 **shìbushì**) phrase in the sentence:

EXAMPLE:

您是不是我们的新老师?
Nín shìbushì wǒménde xīn lǎoshī?
Are you our new teacher?

The third way of asking questions is to use a question word (谁 **shéi** "who," 什么 **shénme** "what," 哪 **nǎ** "which," 为什么 **wèishénme** "why," 多少 **duōshao** "how much," etc.)

EXAMPLES:

谁 来 了? **Shéi lái le?**
Who has come? (= Who is here?)

这些书本多少钱?
Zhèi xiē shūběn duōshao qián?
How much for these books?

To expand a basic sentence, more details can be added progressively, as shown in the examples below.

EXAMPLES:

他是老师。 **Tā shì lǎoshī.**
He is a teacher. (simple sentence)

他是 [一位] 老师。 **Tā shì (yíwèi) lǎoshī.**
He is a teacher. (位 **wèi** = a polite measure word for "person")

他是一位英文老师。
Tā shì yíwèi Yīngwén lǎoshī.
He is an English language teacher. (type of teacher)

他是一位中学英文老师。
Tā shì yíwèi zhōngxué Yīngwén lǎoshī.
He is an English language teacher in a secondary school. (where he works)

HSK Level 1 Vocabulary List

1	爱	ài
2	八	bā
3	爸爸	bàba
4	杯子	bēizi
5	北京	Běijīng
6	本	běn
7	不	bù/bú
8	不客气	búkèqi
9	菜	cài
10	茶	chá
11	吃	chī
12	出租车	chūzūchē
13	打电话	dǎ diànhuà
14	大	dà
15	的	de
16	点	diǎn
17	电脑	diànnǎo
18	电视	diànshì
19	电影	diànyǐng
20	东西	dōngxi
21	都	dōu
22	读	dú
23	对不起	duìbuqǐ
24	多	duō
25	多少	duōshao
26	儿子	érzi
27	二	èr
28	饭馆	fànguǎn
29	飞机	fēijī
30	分钟	fēnzhōng
31	高兴	gāoxìng
32	个	ge
33	工作	gōngzuò
34	狗	gǒu
35	汉语	Hànyǔ
36	好	hǎo
37	喝	hē
38	和	hé

39	很	hěn
40	后面	hòumiàn
41	回	huí
42	会	huì
43	火车站	huǒchēzhàn
44	几	jǐ
45	家	jiā
46	叫	jiào
47	今天	jīntiān
48	九	jiǔ
49	开	kāi
50	看	kàn
51	看见	kànjiàn
52	块	kuài
53	来	lái
54	老师	lǎoshī
55	了	le
56	冷	lěng
57	里	lǐ
58	零	líng
59	六	liù
60	妈妈	māma
61	吗	ma
62	买	mǎi
63	猫	māo
64	没	méi
65	没关系	méi guānxi
66	米饭	mǐfàn
67	明天	míngtiān
68	名字	míngzi
69	哪(儿)	nǎ(r)
70	那(儿)	nà(r)
71	呢	ne
72	能	néng
73	你	nǐ
74	年	nián
75	女儿	nǚ'ér
76	朋友	péngyou

77	漂亮	piàoliang
78	苹果	píngguǒ
79	七	qī
80	钱	qián
81	前面	qiánmiàn
82	请	qǐng
83	去	qù
84	热	rè
85	人	rén
86	认识	rènshi
87	日	rì
88	三	sān
89	商店	shāngdiàn
90	上	shàng
91	上午	shàngwǔ
92	少	shǎo
93	谁	shéi/shuí
94	什么	shénme
95	十	shí
96	时候	shíhòu
97	是	shì
98	书	shū
99	水	shuǐ
100	水果	shuǐguǒ
101	睡觉	shuìjiào
102	说话	shuōhuà
103	四	sì
104	岁	suì
105	他	tā
106	她	tā
107	太	tài
108	天气	tiānqì
109	听	tīng
110	同学	tóngxué
111	喂	wèi
112	我	wǒ
113	我们	wǒmen
114	五	wǔ

115	喜欢	**xǐhuan**		127	星期	**xīngqī**		139	再见	**zàijiàn**
116	下	**xià**		128	学生	**xuésheng**		140	怎么	**zěnme**
117	下午	**xiàwǔ**		129	学习	**xuéxí**		141	怎么样	**zěnmeyàng**
118	下雨	**xià yǔ**		130	学校	**xuéxiào**		142	这(儿)	**zhè(r)**
119	先生	**xiānsheng**		131	一	**yī**		143	中国	**Zhōngguó**
120	现在	**xiànzài**		132	衣服	**yīfu**		144	中午	**zhōngwǔ**
121	想	**xiǎng**		133	医生	**yīshēng**		145	住	**zhù**
122	小	**xiǎo**		134	医院	**yīyuàn**		146	桌子	**zhuōzi**
123	小姐	**xiǎojiě**		135	椅子	**yǐzi**		147	字	**zì**
124	些	**xiē**		136	有	**yǒu**		148	昨天	**zuótiān**
125	写	**xiě**		137	月	**yuè**		149	坐	**zuò**
126	谢谢	**xièxie**		138	在	**zài**		150	做	**zuò**

Common Phrases for HSK Level 1 🎧

Nǐ (Nín) hǎo! 你（您）好！ Hello!, Hi!

Zǎo'ān! 早安！ Good morning.

Zhōngwǔ hǎo! 中午好！ Good afternoon!

Wǎnshàng hǎo! 晚上好！ Good evening!

Zàijiàn! 再见！ Bye!

Xièxie. 谢谢。 Thank you.

Qǐng wèn... 请问… May I ask...

Hěn gāoxīng rènshi nǐ (nín). 很高兴认识你（您）。 Glad to know you.

Wǒ jiào [name]. 我叫… I am [name].

Wǒde míngzi shì [name]. 我的名字是… My name is [name].

Nǐ (nín) chīguòle ma? 你（您）吃过了吗？ Have you eaten?

Wǒmen yìqǐ zǒu ba. 我们一起走吧。 Let's go together.

Jīntiān hěn lěng. 今天很冷。 It is cold today.

Nǐ huì shuō Hànyǔ ma? 你会说汉语吗？ Do you speak Mandarin?

Bù-duō bù-shǎo 不多不少 Exactly (the right amount) / just right

Wǒde tóngxué yǒu yìtiáo xiǎo gǒu. 我的同学有一条小狗。 My classmate has a small dog.

Búkèqi yìqǐ chīfàn ba. 不客气，一起吃饭吧。 You are welcome to join us for a meal.

Kuài jiào chūzūchē! Wǒ gǎn shíjiān. 快叫出租车！我赶时间。 Please call a cab! I am in a rush.

Bàba mǎile yìtái diànnǎo gěi háizi. 爸爸买了一台电脑给孩子。
The father bought his child a computer.

Zhè jǐtiān yǔ xià de hěn dà. 这几天雨下的很大。 It has been raining heavily these few days.

Zhè ge xīngqī wǒ huì qù Bālí. 这个星期我会去巴黎。 I will go to Paris this week.

Zhōngguó rén hěn yǒu xuéwèn. 中国人很有学问。 The Chinese people are very knowledgeable.

Huǒchēzhàn jiù zài fùjìn. 火车站就在附近。 The train station is very near.

HSK Level 2 Vocabulary List

HSK Level 2 vocabulary includes the 150 words from HSK Level 1, plus the 150 words in the table below.

1	吧	ba	37	过	guò	73	妹妹	mèimei
2	白	bái	38	还	hái	74	门	mén
3	百	bǎi	39	孩子	háizi	75	男人	nánrén
4	帮助	bāngzhù	40	好吃	hǎochī	76	您	nín
5	报纸	bàozhǐ	41	号	hào	77	牛奶	niúnǎi
6	比	bǐ	42	黑	hēi	78	女人	nǚrén
7	别	bié	43	红	hóng	79	旁边	pángbiān
8	长	cháng	44	欢迎	huānyíng	80	跑步	pǎobù
9	唱歌	chànggē	45	回答	huídá	81	便宜	piányi
10	出	chū	46	机场	jīchǎng	82	票	piào
11	穿	chuān	47	鸡蛋	jīdàn	83	妻子	qīzi
12	船	chuán	48	件	jiàn	84	起床	qǐchuáng
13	次	cì	49	教室	jiàoshì	85	千	qiān
14	从	cóng	50	姐姐	jiějie	86	晴	qíng
15	错	cuò	51	介绍	jièshào	87	去年	qùnián
16	打篮球	dǎ lánqiú	52	进	jìn	88	让	ràng
17	大家	dàjiā	53	近	jìn	89	上班	shàngbān
18	但是	dànshì	54	就	jiù	90	身体	shēntǐ
19	到	dào	55	觉得	juéde	91	生病	shēngbìng
20	得	de	56	咖啡	kāfēi	92	生日	shēngrì
21	等	děng	57	开始	kāishǐ	93	时间	shíjiān
22	弟弟	dìdi	58	考试	kǎoshì	94	事情	shìqíng
23	第一	dìyī	59	可能	kěnéng	95	手表	shǒubiǎo
24	懂	dǒng	60	可以	kěyǐ	96	手机	shǒujī
25	对	duì	61	课	kè	97	送	sòng
26	房间	fángjiān	62	快	kuài	98	所以	suǒyǐ
27	非常	fēicháng	63	快乐	kuàilè	99	它	tā
28	服务员	fúwùyuán	64	累	lèi	100	踢足球	tī zúqiú
29	高	gāo	65	离	lí	101	题	tí
30	告诉	gàosu	66	两	liǎng	102	跳舞	tiàowǔ
31	哥哥	gēge	67	路	lù	103	外	wài
32	给	gěi	68	旅游	lǚyóu	104	完	wán
33	公共汽车	gōnggòng qìchē	69	卖	mài	105	玩	wán
34	公斤	gōngjīn	70	慢	màn	106	晚上	wǎnshang
35	公司	gōngsī	71	忙	máng	107	为什么	wènshénme
36	贵	guì	72	每	měi	108	问	wèn

109	问题	wèntí	123	药	yào	137	再	zài
110	西瓜	xīguā	124	要	yāo	138	早上	zǎoshang
111	希望	xīwàng	125	也	yě	139	张	zhāng
112	洗	xǐ	126	已经	yǐjīng	140	丈夫	zhàngfu
113	向	xiàng	127	一起	yìqǐ	141	找	zhǎo
114	小时	xiǎoshí	128	意思	yìsi	142	着	zhe
115	笑	xiào	129	阴	yīn	143	真	zhēn
116	新	xīn	130	因为	yīnwèi	144	正在	zhèngzài
117	姓	xìng	131	游泳	yóuyǒng	145	知道	zhīdao
118	休息	xiūxi	132	右边	yòubian	146	准备	zhǔnbèi
119	雪	xuě	133	鱼	yú	147	自行车	zìxíngchē
120	颜色	yánsè	134	元	yuán	148	走	zǒu
121	眼睛	yǎnjing	135	远	yuǎn	149	最	zuì
122	羊肉	yángròu	136	运动	yùndòng	150	左边	zuǒbian

Common Phrases for HSK Level 2 🎧

Huānyíng, huānyíng! 欢迎，欢迎！ Welcome! Welcome!

Máfán nín! 麻烦您！ Sorry to trouble you!

Méi wèntí. 没问题。 No problem / It's OK.

Méi guānxi. 没关系。 It is fine.

Bié shuōle! Wǒ hěn shēngqì! 别说了！我很生气！ Don't talk about it! I'm very angry.

Xīwàng míngtiān gèng hǎo 希望明天更好 Wishing for a better tomorrow

Zhù nín shēngrì kuàilè! 祝您生日快乐！ Happy Birthday!

Duō bǎozhòng shēntǐ! 多保重身体！ Take care of your health!

Zhēn gòu péngyou! 真够朋友！ A friend indeed!

Zìwǒ jièshào 自我介绍 Self-introduction

Méi yìsi / yǒu yìsi 没意思／有意思 Boring; uninteresting / interesting

Néng piànyi yìdiǎn ma? 能便宜一点吗？ Can it be slightly cheaper?

Wǒ kěyǐ jiè nǐ de shū ba? 我可以借你的书吧？ Can I borrow your book?

Tā chángcháng shēngbìng. 她常常生病。 She often falls sick.

Tā de zhàngfu shì yìmíng yìshēng. 她的丈夫是一名医生。 Her husband is a medical doctor.

Wǒ zuò gōnggòng qìchē qù shàngbān. 我坐公共汽车去上班。 I take the bus to work.

Háizi xīnggāocǎiliè de xiàole. 孩子兴高采烈地笑了。 The child smiled merrily.

Wǒ měitiān zǎoshang hē kāfēi. 我每天早上喝咖啡。 I drink coffee every morning.

Nǐ de shǒujī shì zuìxīn de! 你的手机是最新的！ You have the latest smartphone!

Zhège jiàotáng yǐ yǒu 500 nián de lìshǐle. 这个教堂已有500年的历史了。
This church is 500 years old.

"Books to Span the East and West"

Tuttle Publishing was founded in 1832 in the small New England town of Rutland, Vermont [USA]. Our core values remain as strong today as they were then—to publish best-in-class books which bring people together one page at a time. In 1948, we established a publishing outpost in Japan—and Tuttle is now a leader in publishing English-language books about the arts, languages and cultures of Asia. The world has become a much smaller place today and Asia's economic and cultural influence has grown. Yet the need for meaningful dialogue and information about this diverse region has never been greater. Over the past seven decades, Tuttle has published thousands of books on subjects ranging from martial arts and paper crafts to language learning and literature—and our talented authors, illustrators, designers and photographers have won many prestigious awards. We welcome you to explore the wealth of information available on Asia at **www.tuttlepublishing.com**.

Published by Tuttle Publishing, an imprint of Periplus Editions (HK) Ltd.

www.tuttlepublishing.com

Copyright © 2023 by Periplus Editions (HK) Ltd.

ISBN: 978-0-8048-5665-2

Distributed by:

North America, Latin America & Europe
Tuttle Publishing
364 Innovation Drive
North Clarendon, VT 05759-9436 U.S.A.
Tel: 1 (802) 773-8930
Fax: 1 (802) 773-6993
info@tuttlepublishing.com
www.tuttlepublishing.com

Asia Pacific
Berkeley Books Pte. Ltd.
3 Kallang Sector, #04-01
Singapore 349278
Tel: (65) 6741-2178
Fax: (65) 6741-2179
inquiries@periplus.com.sg
www.tuttlepublishing.com

26 25 24 23   10 9 8 7 6 5 4 3 2 1

Printed in Singapore   2203MP

TUTTLE PUBLISHING® is a registered trademark of Tuttle Publishing, a division of Periplus Editions (HK) Ltd.